D0515604

JOKES and RIDDLES

Compiled and Illustrated by

GEORGE L. CARLSON

PLATT & MUNK, *Publishers*
NEW YORK

Made in the United States of America

Library of Congress Catalog Card Number: 59-11876

FOREWORD

ANYONE who has ever watched a small baby is aware that humor appeals strongly to children, starting practically from birth. The chuckling baby quickly grows into the hilariously amused child, experimenting with puns, telling and retelling the newest joke he's heard at school. Humor is as natural to children as breathing, as wholesome as vitamins, and as delightful as ice cream.

This book is designed to give children fun. The jokes and riddles have been specifically chosen for children. They are appropriate in subject matter, and in uniformly good taste. The book is arranged with jokes on the left-hand pages as you open the book and riddles on the right-hand pages, so that the child can enjoy some of each wherever he opens the book. Answers to the riddles start on Page 80.

For a rainy day, for a children's party, for a sick child, for family sharing, or for any other occasion when gaiety is in order, this book will encourage one of your child's favorite pastimes—laughing.

"Waiter! I'm in a hurry! Will the griddle cakes be long?"
"No, sir, round!"

"I started in life without a penny in my pocket!" bragged Mr. Jones.
"And I," replied Mr. Smith, "started in life without a pocket!"

Lawyer: "Among other things, your uncle left you over five hundred clocks."
The Lucky Heir: "Oh, dear! It will take a long time to wind up his estate, won't it?"

RIDDLES

1. Why did the lady go outdoors with her purse open?

2. Why should we hope that the rain keeps up?

3. Why does a rabbit have a shiny nose?

4. What is the hardest work some people do before breakfast?

5. If life is tough, what is something you can always count on?

6. What ant lives in a house?

7. If you gave one friend fifteen cents and another a dime, what time would it be?

8. What makes everyone sick except those who swallow it?

9. Why is a good student always on the run?

10. Where will you find the center of gravity?

"I would like to have copies of your paper for a week back," said the man who came into the newspaper office.
"Why don't you try a porous plaster?"

"Isn't it wonderful how the little chicks get out of their shells?"
"Yes, but it is more wonderful how they get in!"

RIDDLES

11. Why does a tall man eat less than a short one?

12. When does a caterpillar improve in behavior?

13. What is the best way to make a fire with two sticks?

14. What did the bald man say when he got a comb for his birthday?

15. Why is a horse the most unusual eater of all animals?

16. What inventions have helped men get up in the world?

17. What has nothing left but a nose when it loses an eye?

18. What ant is an officer?

19. Why is a musician who can't play well like a counterfeiter?

20. What is the difference between a photograph and a family with whooping cough?

JOKES

Two leopards in the zoo had just finished their lunch, and one sat back and sighed with contentment: "Mm-mm-mm! That just hit the right spots!"

Fred: "Would you sooner lose your life or your money?"
Tom: "Why, my life, of course. I'll need my money for my old age!"

RIDDLES

21. If you were surrounded by twenty lions, fifteen tigers and ten leopards, how would you get away from them?

22. Every morning Farmer Brown had eggs for breakfast, but he didn't own any chickens, and he never got eggs from chickens owned by anyone else. Where did he get the eggs?

23. What did Franklin say when he discovered electricity in lightning?

24. I have cities with no houses, forests without trees, rivers without water. What am I?

25. How can two people stand 2 inches apart without being able to touch each other?

26. What is the only nail a carpenter hates to hit with his hammer?

U. S. Tourist: (in France) "Waiter, bring me some of this — see, here on the menu."
Waiter: "Madam, the orchestra is playing it now."

Elmer: "My Grandpa made a scarecrow so terrible that it frightened every single crow off the place!"
Hiram: "You think *THAT'S* something! I made one that scared them so much they brought back the corn they stole last year!"

RIDDLES

27. What is it that every child spends much time making, yet no one can ever see it when made?

28. What can you break with a whisper more easily than you can with a hammer?

29. I am something that always increases, the more I am shared with others. What do you think I am?

30. What city is for telegraph operators?

31. Why must it be difficult to eat soup with a mustache?

32. What is the coldest row in the theater?

33. Why is a river rich?

34. What's the difference between a ghost and a lame sailor walking?

35. Why are flowers lazy?

36. Why does a dog wear more clothes in summer than in winter?

"You say there's one thing you can't eat for breakfast?"
"Yes, supper!"

Diner: "Have you any wild duck?"
Waiter: "No, sir, but we can take a tame one and make him real mad at you!"

"Do you have hot and cold water in this hotel?" inquired the visitor.
"Yes, ma'am," replied the clerk, "hot in the summer and cold in the winter."

RIDDLES

37. What would you have if a bird got caught in a lawn mower?

38. What wheel goes 'round without touching the ground?

39. Why is a railroad engine like the family wash?

40. What is always broken before it is used?

41. When do broken bones make themselves useful?

42. What age is important to an automobile?

43. Who are the best bookkeepers?

44. What has a foot and a head but can't walk or think.

45. What age is served at breakfast?

46. What should we give people who are too breezy?

JOKES

Bess: "I don't see how football players ever get clean!"
Tess: "Well, what do you suppose the scrub teams are for?"

Shopper: "How much are these tomatoes?"
Grocer: "Forty cents a pound!"
Shopper: "Did you raise them yourself?"
Grocer: "Yes, ma'am — I did! They were only thirty-five cents yesterday!"

RIDDLES

47. When is an artist very unhappy?

48. What runs all around the cow pasture, yet never moves?

49. What is the difference between a tailor and a stable boy?

50. What is the best way to get a duck for dinner?

51. Why does the moon go to the bank?

52. When do your teeth sound just like your tongue?

53. What age do people get stuck on?

54. Who makes light of his work?

55. What binds two people together, yet only touches one?

56. At what age will vessels ride safely?

Diner: "Do you serve crabs here?"
Waiter: "We serve anyone; sit right down."

Billy Goat: (eating a cook book in a pile of rubbish) "This book sure tastes good! I never ate anything more delicious!"

Customer: "That chicken I bought yesterday had no wish-bone!"
Butcher: "Ah, ma'am! It was a happy and contented chicken and had nothing to wish for!"

RIDDLES

57. Which of the stars should be subject to the game laws?

58. What musical instrument invites you to fish?

59. Spell "enemy" in three letters.

60. When are stockings like carpenters' aprons?

61. Why are pianos noble in character?

62. What is it that is lower with a head than without one?

63. What happens to a man who starts home to dinner and misses his train?

64. What shoemaker makes shoes without using any leather?

65. What is the difference between a mirror and a boy who chatters nonsense?

66. If you were locked up in a room with nothing but a baseball bat, how would you get out?

JOKES

Fussy Lady Patient: "Do you think raw oysters are healthy?"
Weary Doctor: "I never knew one to complain!"

Sally Ann: "Mother, how long is it to my birthday?"
Mother: "Not very long, dear!"
Sally Ann: "Well, is it time for me to begin being a good girl?"

Grandma: "And were you a good little girl at church this morning, Betsy?"
Betsy: "Oh, yes, Grandma! A nice man offered me a plate full of money, but I said, 'No, thank you, sir!' "

RIDDLES

67. What colors did the artist use in his picture of the storm at sea?

68. What is the difference between a light in a cave and a dance in an inn?

69. Why should the highest apple on a tree be the best one?

70. What city is noted for the greatest feat of all strength ever performed in the United States?

71. What do they have in Brooklyn that they haven't got in Manhattan?

72. I have a head and a tail, but no body. What am I?

73. Why is it useless to send a telegram to Washington today?

74. What is a sure way to grow fat?

Little Mortimer: "I et six eggs for breakfast this morning."
Teacher: "You mean 'ate', don't you?"
Little Mortimer: "Well, maybe it was eight I et."

Mop and whisk broom salesman to little boy:
"Sonny, is your mother at home?"
Salesman: (after knocking for some time and getting no answer) "I thought you said she was at home!"
Little Boy: "Yes, sir, but I don't live here!"

75. What did the ghost have for breakfast?

76. What ship has no captain but two mates?

77. When can you name a dog "Hickory"?

78. What is the worst kind of sipping?

79. How can you find a "chip off the old block"?

80. Why doesn't Sweden send to other countries for cattle?

81. Which are the most contented birds?

82. Why does the farmer put a porcelain egg under the hen?

83. Why is a love of the ocean like curiosity?

84. How can you benefit by having a paper of pins?

85. What keys are too big to carry in your pocket?

JOKES

Teacher: "Davie, this homework looks like your father's handwriting!"
Davie: "Sure, I used his fountain pen!"

Jim: "I saw something last night I'll never get over!"
Joe: "What was that?"
Jim: "The moon."

Freddie: "Why are you crying?"
Billy: "Because Jimmy hit me."
Freddie: "Why did he hit you?"
Billy: "Because I was crying!"

86. Why do you forget a tooth after it's pulled out?

87. What is the surest way to keep fish from smelling?

88. Why should a fisherman always be wealthy?

89. Why should spiders make good outfielders?

90. How can you get into a locked cemetery at night?

91. What do all ships weigh, regardless of size?

92. What is better than to give credit where credit is due?

93. What nut lives on a sandy shore?

94. What nut reminds you of a large strong box?

95. What is better than presence of mind in an automobile accident?

96. Why does a bald-headed man have no use for keys?

JOKES

Hungry Sailor: (at mealtime) "I'm hungry enough to eat a horse!"

Second Sailor: "Don't worry! That's what we're getting in a few minutes!"

Traveler: "How much will you charge to take my baggage to Canal Street?"

Taxi Driver: "Half a dollar for you, sir. Your baggage goes free."

Traveler: "Okay, then. You just take the baggage, and I'll walk."

RIDDLES

97. What is worse than a giraffe with a sore throat?

98. What is the sculptor's favorite cake?

99. Why are money and a secret alike?

100. What can a stingy man best part with?

101. What kind of ice is not in your icebox? (We hope!)

102. When is a department store like a boat?

103. How old would you be if you were very, very fat?

104. No man wants me, but once he's got me, no man wants to lose me. What am I?

105. Why did Dad tiptoe past the medicine chest when he got in late last night?

106. A duck, a frog and a skunk went to the circus. Tickets were a dollar. Who got in, and who didn't?

107. Is there a word in the English language that contains all the vowels?

"Isn't it bad luck to have a cat follow you?"
"It depends. Are you a man or a mouse?"

Mother: "What are you looking for, Johnny?"
Johnny: "Nothing."
Mother: "You'll find it in the box where the candy was."

Kind Old Lady: (to tramp) "Has anybody ever offered you work?"
Tramp: "Only once, lady. Except for that, I've met only with kindness."

RIDDLES

108. Why did twenty-four people get up and leave the table on June 17th at Delmonico's famous restaurant?

109. When the doctor wanted to get his report published, where was it printed?

110. What is always filled when in use and empty when at rest?

111. What is it that can be broken without being hit or dropped?

112. How might you be completely sleepless for seven days and still not lack any rest?

113. I occur once in every minute, twice in every moment, and yet never in a hundred thousand years. What am I?

114. What is found in the middle of both America and Australia?

115. When you look around on a cold winter day, what do you see on every hand?

116. What is it that lives in winter, dies in summer, and grows with its roots upwards?

JOKES

"If you wash your face, I'll give you a piece of chocolate," said Grandma, "and if you wash behind your ears, I'll give you two pieces."

"Grandma," replied little Davie, "maybe I'd better have a bath!"

Teacher: "If you have ten potatoes and must divide them equally among seven persons, how would you do it?"

Johnny: "I'd mash them!"

RIDDLES

117. What word can be pronounced quicker by adding another syllable to it?

118. What word of five letters has six left after you take two away?

119. In the word "cloves," why are "c" and "s," although separated, closely attached?

120. If ten birds were sitting on a telephone wire and you shot one, how many would remain?

121. The first part of an odd number is removed and it becomes even. What number is it?

122. If a cork and a bottle cost $2.10, and the bottle costs $2.00 more than the cork, what does the cork cost?

123. Soldiers mark time with their feet. What does the same thing with its hands?

124. If two San Francisco telegraph operators were married, what would they become?

125. What did a mother sardine say to her baby sardine when they saw a submarine?

JOKES

"Those are rather loud socks!"
"Yes, I know, but they keep my feet from falling asleep!"

Diner: "Waiter, this soup is cold. Bring me some that's hot!"
Waiter: "What do you want me to do, burn my thumb?"

Customer: (in roadside lunchroom) "One cup of coffee without cream."
Waiter: "I can't give it to you without cream, but I can give it to you without milk."

RIDDLES

126. What letter is never found in the alphabet?

127. Why are fishermen such good correspondents?

128. Why is a poor joke like an unsharpened pencil?

129. What is worse than finding a worm in an apple?

130. What is the best thing to take when you are run-down?

131. Which man always finds things dull?

132. What is the difference between an old penny and a new nickel?

133. How does the letter "A" help a deaf woman?

134. Why are fish well educated?

135. What vegetable needs a plumber?

Visitor: "And what's your boy going to be when he finishes his education?"
Discouraged Parent: "A very, very old man, I think!"

Student: "But I don't think I deserve a zero on this paper!"
Professor: "Neither do I, but it's the lowest mark I can give you."

RIDDLES

136. When is a piece of wood like a king?

137. What is the difference between a hill and a pill?

138. What is the difference between a poor man and a featherbed?

139. Why is a baseball game like a biscuit?

140. What is a waffle?

141. Why is a banana peel like a sweater?

142. When is music like an icy sidewalk?

143. No matter how smart you are, what is the only thing you will always overlook?

144. What should a man know before trying to teach tricks to a dog?

145. What do you use twice in every day, four times in every week, and only once in a year?

146. If a man smashed a clock, could he be accused of killing time?

JOKES

Pete Pelican: "That's a fine fish you have there!"
Pat Pelican: "Well, it fills the bill!"

Fussy Old Lady: "Those sausages you sent me were meat at one end and corn meal at the other!"
Butcher: "Yes, ma'am, in these hard times it's difficult to make both ends meat!"

Fussy Lady: (shopping in fish market) "I don't like the looks of that codfish!"
Fish Dealer: "Well, if it's looks you're after, why don't you buy a goldfish?"

147. If your dog started to chew up your pocket dictionary, what should you do?

148. What should you do if you always get sick at night before a trip?

149. What's a good thing to do when you find you have a short circuit in the wiring of your car?

150. When can you kick about a gift?

151. Why is a crossword puzzle like a quarrel?

152. After the rain falls, when does it rise again?

153. Why are clocks so shy?

154. What falls but doesn't break, and what breaks but doesn't fall?

155. Why would you take a ruler to bed with you at night?

156. Why do you comb your hair before going to bed?

157. What kind of clothing lasts the longest?

Grandfather looked very different to little 4-year old Betsy when he came on a recent visit. He had shaved off his big bushy beard and it was the first time Betsy had seen him with a smooth clean face.

"Oh, Grandpa!" she exclaimed. "Whose head have you got on?"

Fond Father: "Now, sonny, if you are a good boy today, I'll give you this nice, new, shiny penny."

Sonny: "Aw, Dad, can't you make it a battered old quarter?"

158. Why is a dentist unhappy at work?

159. Who are the three unluckiest girls in the world?

160. What kind of trees should you use at night?

161. What is the biggest jewel in the world?

162. When is silence apt to get wet?

163. What stays hot even if you put it in a refrigerator?

164. Why must a dishonest man stay indoors?

165. Why is a clock like a river?

166. When can the alphabet be shortened?

167. What is the surest way to double your dollar?

168. Why is the Senate like a book?

JOKES

Teacher: "Yes, Frank, what is it?"
Frank: "I don't want to scare you, but Dad said if I don't get better marks soon, someone is due for a spanking!"

Customer: "Do you guarantee this hair restorer?"
Clerk: "Better than that, sir—we give a comb with every bottle!"

Frankie: "Did you hear that Jones is making a hundred dollars a night playing the violin?"
Johnnie: "Imagine! Twenty-five dollars a string!"
Frankie: "He should play a harp!"

RIDDLES

169. How do sailors get their clothes clean?

170. My hair is coming out — what can I get to keep it in?

171. Which is the strongest day of the week?

172. When is a hat not a hat?

173. What runs around town all day and lies down all night with its tongue hanging out?

174. What is the difference between a sixteen-ounce baby and a man working busily on his typewriter?

175. When may a man's coat pocket be empty and yet have something in it?

176. What is the difference between a man looking at Niagara Falls, a man that is not looking at Niagara Falls, and a ham sandwich?

177. How many times can 18 be subtracted from 180?

178. What word is always pronounced wrong?

JOKES

Proud Mother: "Yes, he's fourteen months old now,—and he's been walking since he was eight months old!"
Visitor: "Really? He must be awfully tired!"

Molly: "And Santa brought me this lovely woolen sweater!"
Polly: "But it isn't wool! It has a label marked 'cotton' on it!"
Molly: "Yes, I know—that's to fool the moths!"

179. What did one penny say to the other?

180. How long will an eight-day clock run without winding?

181. What is the difference between the world's heavyweight boxing champion and a man with a cold?

182. What is it everyone would like to have, yet wants to get rid of as soon as he gets it?

183. What's the difference between a dog losing his hair and a man painting a small building?

184. What kind of party would the prisoners in a jail like?

185. What does a lamp post become when the lamp is removed?

186. What wears covering in the summer and goes bare all winter?

187. What bird is present at every meal?

188. What do women look for, but never wish to find?

Paymaster: "How long have you been working here?"
Office Boy: "Ever since the day the boss threatened to fire me!"

Customer: "With as little hair as I have, do I pay a full price for a haircut?"
Barber: "Yes, maybe a bit more. We usually charge double when we have to hunt for the hair!"

Mom: (to the new hired girl) "Hilda, have you given the goldfish fresh water today?"
Hilda: "No, ma'am. They haven't finished the water I gave them yesterday."

RIDDLES

189. How can you make money fast?

190. What keeps the moon in place?

191. What two letters of the alphabet contain nothing?

192. What does an envelope say when it is licked?

193. What is it that you cannot see, but it is always before you?

194. Name five things that contain milk.

195. What is the most striking thing in the way of mantel ornaments?

196. Why is a rooster on a fence like a penny?

197. Why does a calf wag its tail?

198. What resembles one-half of a cheese?

199. Why do the carpenters believe there is no such thing as stone?

JOKES

"Why don't you finish your alphabet soup, Danny?" asked his mother. "There are a few letters left in your plate."
"I know," answered Danny, "but they spell S-P-I-N-A-C-H!"

Harry: "That cake you're eating looks good."
Barry: "It *IS* good."
Harry: "It makes my mouth water."
Barry: "To show you what a good guy I am, here's a blotter."

RIDDLES

200. Why is a loaf of bread four weeks old like a rat running into a hole?

201. If a burglar got into a cellar, would the coal shoot (chute)?

202. What bridge has never been walked on?

203. Where did Julius Caesar go on his thirty-ninth birthday?

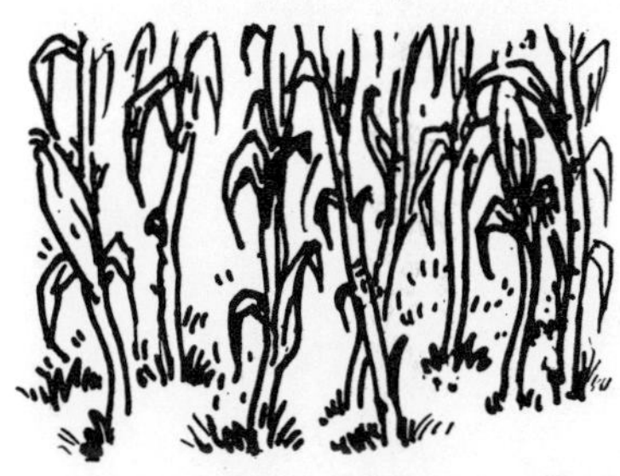

204. Why are every man's pants too short?

205. Why does more corn grow in crooked rows than in straight ones?

206. When is a man over head and ears in debt?

207. Why is the army not going to have bayonets any longer?

208. What is the queerest animal there is?

209. What is hard to beat?

JOKES

A card appeared on the front window of a house on our block: PIANO FOR SALE
Next day a card appeared in the window next door:
HURRAH!

Teacher: "Do you know the name of an animal that travels great distances?"
Smart Pupil: "Yes, a goldfish! It travels around the globe!"

RIDDLES

210. Why is an eclipse like a father spanking his boy?

211. Why do we usually find a painter's studio as hot as an oven?

212. Which is the most generous animal in the world?

213. When is a fish like a bird?

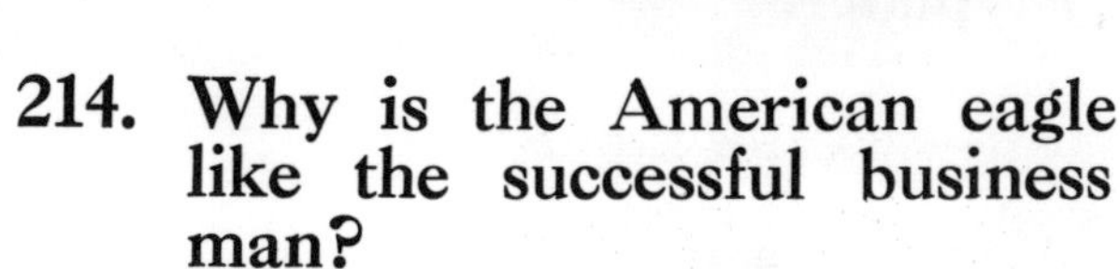

214. Why is the American eagle like the successful business man?

215. When is a gardener like a story writer?

216. Put three ducks into a crate, and what would you have?

217. What should be looked into?

218. What increases its value one-half when turned upside down?

219. What can you make best in a hurry?

"What kind of paper should I use when I make my kite?"
"Flypaper."

Teacher: "Georgie, what is a synonym?"
Georgie: "A synonym is a word you use when you can't spell the other one."

"I hear old General Sputterfuss has stomach trouble. What's the cause of it?"
"Oh, just things in general!"

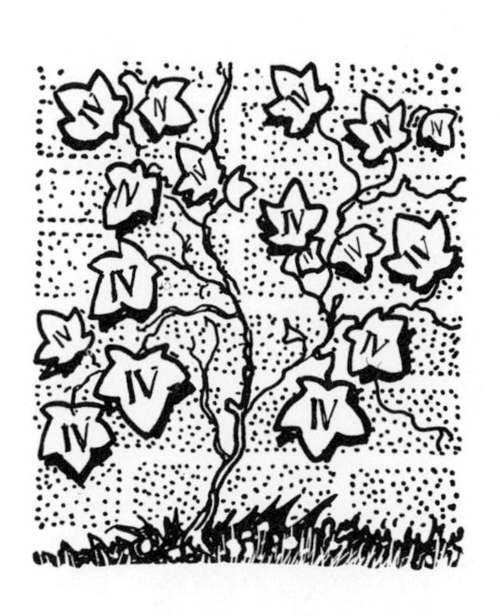

220. When you examine a dog's lungs with the X-ray, what do you find?

221. When is a dog's tail like a toll-gate?

222. What plant stands for number four anywhere?

223. When is a boy with a cold in his chest *not* a boy?

224. What character in history did a certain person mention when he asked the servant to put coal on the fire?

225. What is the best way to keep loafers from standing on street corners?

226. A woman had five children. Half of them were boys; what were the other half?

227. Why is a lame dog like a schoolboy adding six and seven together?

228. What professional man generally shows his teeth to a customer?

229. What statue on the Court House does the North Pole remind you of?

"Are you crazy if you talk to yourself?"
"No, but you are if you listen!"

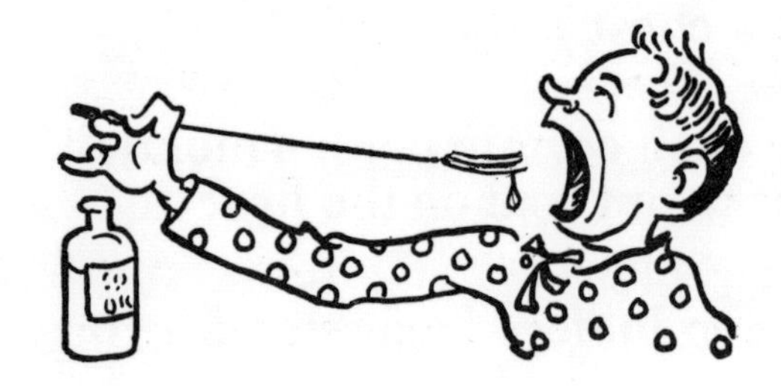

Mother: "What do you want to take your cod liver oil with, this morning, Elmer?"
Elmer: "A fork."

High School Boy: (to clerk) "I'd like a box of pencils, please?"
Clerk: "Hard or soft?"
High School Boy: "Soft. They're for writing love letters."

230. What is that which has never been felt, seen or heard, never existed and still has a name?

231. What is the difference between a fashionable man and a tired dog?

232. What is the difference between a man with an unnatural voice and a woman with unnatural teeth?

233. Why does a farmer, in his field in springtime, remind you of an ocean steamship?

234. What is the difference between a special policeman and an old hat?

235. What eater was all day at the lunch counter without eating a thing?

JOKES

Theater Usher: "How far down do you want to sit, madam?"
Lady: "Why, all the way, of course!"

The best way to drive a nail without mashing your fingers is to hold the hammer with both hands.

Little Betsy: (at dancing school) "You'd be a fine dancer except for two things!"
Bobby: "What?"
Betsy: "Your feet!"

RIDDLES

236. Why are lawyers like crows?

237. What is the best thing to do in a hurry?

238. What is the favorite fruit of history?

239. Why is the letter "P" like a Roman Emperor?

240. Why would you put a blanket on a colt?

241. Use me well, and I am everybody; scratch my back and I am nobody. What am I?

242. Why is a cat like the world?

243. How does a very little fish get the right idea of business?

244. Why are satchels like handcuffs?

245. Who was the strongest man in the Bible?

JOKES

Teacher: "I hope I didn't see you looking at Freddie's book, Tommy!"
Tommy: "I hope you didn't, too!"

Artist: (to an onlooker) "That, sir, is a cow grazing!"
Onlooker: "Where is the grass?"
Artist: "The cow has eaten it!"
Onlooker: "But where is the cow?"
Artist: "You don't suppose she'd be fool enough to stay there after she'd eaten all the grass, do you?"

Stranger: (to farmer) "Why are you using that steam roller on your fields?"
Farmer: "I'm raising mashed potatoes."

246. What two animals go everywhere you go?

247. What is the difference between a hungry man and a greedy man?

248. Why did the boy "stand on the burning deck"?

249. When can 125 pounds go for a four-cent stamp?

250. Which is more correct to say—5 plus 4 *is* 11, or *are* 11?

251. Why is twice ten like twice eleven?

252. Where is Minute Street?

253. What is it we often see made, but never see *after* it is made?

254. Why does a golfer wear two pairs of pants?

255. Why is the ocean so restless?

256. When is water most likely to escape?

The class was having a lesson in geography, and the teacher asked: "Johnny, where's the largest corn grown?"
Johnny: "On Pop's little toe!"

'Got a match? I lost a penny."
"No, but my dog will find the (s)cent!"

"Betsy, have you filled the salt shakers?"
"Not yet, Mother, it's hard pushing the salt through these little holes!"

257. When is a fly one of the grocer's best customers?

258. What flower most resembles a cow's mouth?

259. What is the cheapest feature on your face?

260. What is it which *stands* fast, yet sometimes *runs* fast?

261. When you listen to a drum, why are you a good judge of music?

262. Why is a locksmith like a musician?

263. Why is a fruit cake like the ocean?

264. What is it that is remarkable about a yardstick?

265. When is a pint of milk not a pint?

"Oh, that's only a little green snake!"
"Yes, but maybe it's just as dangerous as a ripe one!"

"This liniment makes my arm smart!"
"Why not rub some on your head?"

"Mom! Do you remember that vase you always worried I would break?"
"Yes, what about it?"
"Your worries are over!"

RIDDLES

266. When is a clock cruel?

267. What was there to drink at the beginning of Time?

268. What is a country seat?

269. Why did the farmer feed his cow money?

270. Have you heard the story of the ear of corn? No?

271. When did Washington first take a carriage?

272. Why is an old chair that has a new bottom on it like a paid bill?

273. Where did they put the chickens on board the ship?

274. Why is a goose like an elephant's trunk?

275. What tradesman should be most popular?

"Johnny," asked the teacher, "what are the seasons?"
Johnny: "Baseball, football, skating, and vacation!"

"What do you find the most difficult on the piano?"
"Paying the instalments!"

Young wife: (at her first ball game) "Let's go, dear."
Hubby: "Why?"
Wife: "That same man was on third base when we came in!"

RIDDLES

276. Why is a cent like a cow?

277. Where should you feel for the poor?

278. Why is the job of being President like a back tooth?

279. Who dares to sit before the Queen with his cap on?

280. Why does Santa Claus always go down the chimney?

281. Instead of complaining when it rains, we should do as they do in Spain, and what is that?

282. Why is the bookkeeper's account book like the sculptor's studio?

283. If we were to bore a hole exactly through the earth, starting from Dublin, and you went in at that end, where would you come out?

284. What is the difference between a blind man and a sailor in prison?

285. What is unable to think or speak, yet tells the truth to all the world?

JOKES

"Where's the paper plate that was under your pie?"
"Oh, I thought that was the lower crust!"

Teacher: "What is wind?"
Little Betsy: "Air in a hurry!"

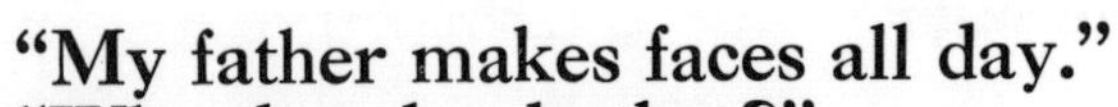

"My father makes faces all day."
"Why does he do that?"
"Because he works in a clock factory."

RIDDLES

286. What is too much for one, enough for two, but nothing at all for three?

287. What is the difference between a summer dress in winter and an extracted tooth?

288. Why should a ship's officer never put his chronometer under his pillow?

289. How can you always have what you please?

290. Why is tallow like a busybody?

291. Why are seasick excursionists like stubborn Congressmen?

292. What is the best way to kill time in the winter?

293. How is it that summer goes by so quickly?

294. What burns to keep a secret?

295. What is that of which the common sort is best?

296. Why is a stupid servant like a church bell?

Book Store Clerk: "This book will do half your work."
Customer: "Give me two!"

"What would you do if you found a dollar bill in your pants' pocket?"
"Look to see whose pants I had on!"

Willie: "I've added these figures ten times now, sir."
Professor: "Good boy!"
Willie: "And here are the ten answers!"

RIDDLES

297. Though I danced at a ball, yet I am nothing at all. What am I?

298. Why does a dressmaker never lose her hooks?

299. Why does a man, just shaved, look like a brute?

300. What's the difference between the bus and the sidewalk?

301. Why did Johnny's teacher put him in the B class?

302. What tree bears the most toothsome fruit?

303. What does the sun do when it sets?

304. In what month do women talk the least?

305. Why are tallest people always the laziest?

306. Why is a ropemaker like a poet?

Salesman: "This tonic will grow hair on a billiard ball!"
Customer: "Who wants hair on a billiard ball?"

"In the summer I get up as soon as the first ray of sun comes in at my window."
"Isn't that rather early?"
"No, my room faces west."

Bob: "We've got a hen down on our farm that lays white eggs!"
Bill: "What's so wonderful about that?"
Bob: "Can *YOU* do it?"

307. Why is there not a minute that we can call our own?

308. When is it that a chair doesn't like you?

309. What tongue is it that is likely to give you trouble, and yet does not speak a word?

310. Which is the day of the year when you should go forward?

311. What is the difference between a comedian outside of a theater and one inside?

312. If a tree were to break the panes of a window, what would they say?

313. What should you do if you woke up in the night, and heard a mouse squeaking?

314. What is the best way to make time go fast?

315. What are the best seats in the opera house?

316. Why is thunder like an onion?

Doctor: "Don't you know my hours are from 2 to 4 P.M.?"
Patient: "Yes, but the dog that bit me didn't!"

"If *I* had a thousand men and *YOU* had a thousand men, and *WE* had a war, who would win?"
"I give up!"
"*I* win!—*YOU* just gave up!"

Ship's Officer: "How's your insomnia?"
Ship's Cook: "It's getting worse. I can't even sleep when it's time to get up!"

317. What is the most warlike nation?

318. Why are frames put around tomato plants?

319. What is the difference between truth and eggs?

320. How can you remove "A" from the alphabet?

321. How can one tell the naked truth?

322. What ailment troubles the oak tree most?

323. Why is a well-trained horse like a generous man?

324. Why shouldn't you have a short walking stick?

325. If a little dog should lose his tail, where would he get another?

326. What is that which, although only six inches long and three inches wide, contains a solid foot?

"So you have a new baby sister, Richard; what's her name?"
"I don't know—can't understand a word she says!"

"When I went into the house late last night I fell against the piano."
"Did it hurt you?"
"No, I fell on the soft pedal."

Fussy Diner in a Restaurant: "Yes, waiter, I'll have lamb chops and mashed potatoes. And make the chops lean!"
"Yes, sir. Which way, sir?"

327. What is the difference between a man dodging footwear that is being thrown at him and a man chasing some ducks out of his pond?

328. When is longhand quicker and more accurate than shorthand?

329. What makes a pair of shoes?

330. When is a shoemaker like a doctor?

331. Why is a stout man apt to be melancholy?

332. Why is a famous soprano singer like a jeweler?

333. What is larger than a nutmeg?

334. When is a cigar like dried beef?

335. When does a boy sneeze three times?

336. What would contain all the snuff in the world?

JOKES

Comedian: "Look here, I do object to going on right after the monkey act."
Stage Manager: "You're right. They'll think it's an encore."

Johnnie: (buying new shoes) "What is that?"
Clerk: "That's a shoe horn!"
Johnnie: "Well, let's hear you blow it!"

Tommy: "What did you get that little silver medal for?"
Jimmy: "For singing."
Tommy: "And—what did you get that big gold medal for?"
Jimmy: "For stopping."

RIDDLES

337. What is the best form for a soldier?

338. When is a soldier not half a soldier?

339. Do big ships like the Titanic sink very often?

340. Why is it best to tell a story with a hammer?

341. When is a young lady's cheek not a cheek?

342. Why do young ladies "put up" their hair at night?

343. Why is a woman with twins like a soldier on guard duty?

344. When does a young lady resemble a nut?

345. What headlines do women always notice?

346. What would you do if your pal told you he killed a lion in Africa 13 feet long?

"You call *that* a police dog! It doesn't look like one!"
"Oh, he's in the secret service!"

Salesman: "There you are, mister, that hat fits perfectly. How does it feel?"
Customer: "Okay, unless my ears get tired!"

Restaurant Owner: (to careless waiter) "And during dinner, you spilled soup on the Admiral's coat!!"
Waiter: "But the Admiral didn't mind, sir. It was Navy Bean Soup!"

RIDDLES

347. What is the difference between a legal document and a man who has just had a big meal?

348. You can hang me up on the wall, but if you take me down, you cannot hang me up again. What am I?

349. There were sixteen ears of corn in a barrel. A rabbit came each night and carried away three ears. How long did it take him to empty the barrel?

350. How did the boy feel when he was kept after school for bad spelling?

351. If you were invited to a dinner, and found nothing on the table but a beet, what would you say?

352. Why is it that a hen always crosses *over* the wagon marks in the road?

353. Why is a washerwoman like Saturday?

354. Can you add two figures to 19 and make it *less* than 20?

355. How may bookkeeping be taught in a lesson of four words?

356. Why didn't the dog want to go into the ark?

ANSWERS TO RIDDLES

1. Because she expected some change in the weather.
2. So it won't come down.
3. Because its powder puff is at the other end.
4. Getting up.
5. Your fingers.
6. Occupant.
7. A quarter to two.
8. Flattery.
9. Because he is always pursuing his studies.
10. At the letter "V."
11. Because he makes a little go a long way.
12. Whenever he turns over a new leaf.
13. Make sure one of them is a match.
14. "Thank you very much. I'll never part with it."
15. Because he eats best when there isn't a bit in his mouth.
16. The elevator and the alarm clock.
17. Noise.
18. Commandant.
19. Because he is always passing out bad notes.
20. One is a fac-simile, and the other a sick family.
21. Stop the merry-go-round and get off.
22. From his ducks—they were ducks' eggs!
23. Nothing. He was too shocked.
24. A map.
25. Close the door between them.
26. His fingernail.
27. Noise.
28. A secret.
29. Happiness.

ANSWERS TO RIDDLES

30. Electricity.
31. Because it is quite a strain.
32. Z - Row (zero).
33. Because it always has two banks.
34. One is a hobgoblin and the other is a gob hobblin'.
35. You'll always find them in beds.
36. In winter he wears a coat. In summer he wears a coat, and pants (for breath).
37. Shredded tweet (wheat).
38. A ferris wheel.
39. Because both of them go on a line.
40. An egg.
41. When they begin to knit.
42. Mileage.
43. People who never return the books you lend to them.
44. A hill.
45. Sausage.
46. The air.
47. When he draws a long face.
48. The fence.
49. One mends a tear, and the other tends a mare.
50. Go jump in the lake.
51. To change quarters.
52. When they chatter.
53. Mucilage.
54. The electrician.
55. A wedding ring.
56. Anchorage.
57. Shooting stars.

ANSWERS TO RIDDLES

58. Cast-a-net.
59. No, it's not "N-M-E." Try again—it's "F-O-E."
60. When they have nails in them.
61. Because they are upright and grand.
62. A pillow.
63. He catches it after he gets home.
64. A blacksmith makes horseshoes.
65. A mirror reflects without talking, and the boy talks without reflecting.
66. Strike one, strike two, strike three, YOU'RE OUT!
67. The wind "blue" and the waves "rose."
68. One is a taper in a cavern, and the other is a caper in a tavern.
69. Because it is a tip-top apple.
70. Wheeling, West Virginia.
71. The other end of the Brooklyn Bridge.
72. A coin.
73. Because he is dead.
74. Raise hogs.
75. Ghost toasties with evaporated milk.
76. Courtship.
77. When he has a rough bark.
78. Gossiping.
79. Just "axe" the block.
80. Because she keeps a good Stockholm (stock home).
81. Crows, because they never complain without caws (cause).
82. To set a good example (egg-sample).
83. Because it has sent many a boy out to sea (see).

ANSWERS TO RIDDLES

84. It will give you many good points.
85. A donkey, a monkey and a turkey.
86. Because it goes right out of your head.
87. Cut off their noses.
88. Because all his business is net profit.
89. Because they always catch flies.
90. Use a skeleton key.
91. Anchors.
92. Give cash.
93. Beechnut (beach-nut).
94. Chestnut.
95. Absence of body.
96. Because he has lost his locks.
97. A centipede with sore feet.
98. Marble cake.
99. Because both are hard to keep.
100. A comb.
101. Mice.
102. When it has sales (sails).
103. The same age you are now.
104. A bald head.
105. Because he was afraid he would wake up the sleeping pills.
106. The duck got in because she had a bill. The frog got in on his green back. But the poor old skunk couldn't get in because he had only a (s)cent, and it was a BAD one.
107. Unquestionably.
108. They were through eating.
109. In the news of the weak (week).

ANSWERS TO RIDDLES

110. A shoe.
111. A promise.
112. By sleeping nights.
113. The letter "M."
114. The letter "R."
115. Gloves.
116. An icicle.
117. Quick.
118. Six-ty.
119. Because there is love between them.
120. None, because they would all fly away.
121. (S)even.
122. The cork costs 5 cents and the bottle costs $2.05.
123. A watch.
124. Western Union.
125. "Don't be afraid; it's only a can of people."
126. The one you mail in the Post Office.
127. Because they're always dropping a line.
128. Because it has no point.
129. Finding half a worm.
130. The number of the car that hit you.
131. The scissors grinder.
132. Four cents.
133. It makes her H-E-A-R.
134. Because they travel in schools.
135. A leek (leak).
136. When it is made into a ruler.
137. A hill is hard to get up, but a pill is hard to get down.
138. One is "hard up" and the other is soft down.

ANSWERS TO RIDDLES

139. Because its success depends on the batter.
140. A pancake with a non-skid tread.
141. Because you can slip on both.
142. If you don't C sharp, you will B flat.
143. Your nose.
144. More than the dog.
145. The letter "E."
146. Not if the clock struck first.
147. Take the words right out of his mouth.
148. Start a day earlier.
149. Just lengthen it.
150. When it's a football.
151. Because one word leads to another.
152. In dew (due) time.
153. Because they always hold their hands before their faces.
154. Night falls but doesn't break. Day breaks but doesn't fall.
155. To find out how long you slept.
156. To make a good impression on the pillow.
157. Underwear, because it is never worn out.
158. Because he looks down in the mouth.
159. Mis-chance, Mis-fortune, and Mis-hap.
160. Shoe trees.
161. A baseball diamond.
162. When it reigns (rains).
163. Pepper.
164. So no one will ever find him out.
165. Because it won't run long without winding.
166. When "U" (you) and "I" are one.

ANSWERS TO RIDDLES

167. Fold it.
168. Because it has pages.
169. They throw them overboard and they are washed ashore.
170. A paper bag.
171. Sunday, because all the rest are week days.
172. When it becomes a girl.
173. Your shoe.
174. One weighs a pound and the other pounds away.
175. When it has a hole in it.
176. One is seeing the mist and the other is missing the scene. The ham sandwich?—Oh, that's where you bite!
177. Only once, because any later subtractions would not be from 180, but from a smaller number.
178. W-R-O-N-G, of course.
179. "Let's get together and make some cents (sense)."
180. It won't run at all without winding.
181. One knows his blows and the other blows his nose.
182. A good appetite.
183. One sheds his coat and the other coats his shed.
184. Open house.
185. A lamp-lighter.
186. A tree.
187. A swallow.
188. A run in their stockings.
189. Nail it to the floor.
190. Its beams.
191. M. T. (empty).
192. It shuts up and says nothing.

ANSWERS TO RIDDLES

193. The future.
194. Butter, cheese, ice cream, and two cows.
195. A clock.
196. Because his head's on one side and his tail's on the other.
197. Because it wants to.
198. The other half.
199. Because they never saw it.
200. Because you can see its tail (it's stale).
201. No, but the kindling wood (would).
202. The bridge of your nose.
203. Into his fortieth year.
204. Because two feet of his legs stick out.
205. There are more crooked rows.
206. When he wears a wig that is not paid for.
207. They are long enough.
208. An author—his tail (tale) comes out of his head.
209. A hard-boiled egg.
210. Because it's a hiding of the sun (son).
211. Because it is there he makes his bread.
212. A skunk, because it gives everyone passing a (s)cent.
213. When it takes a fly.
214. Because he is found wherever there is a dollar.
215. When he works up his plot.
216. A box of quackers.
217. A mirror.
218. Figure 6.
219. Haste.
220. The seat of his pants.
221. When he stops a waggin' (wagon).

222. Ivy (IV).
223. When he is a little horse (hoarse).
224. Philip the Great (Fill up the grate).
225. Give them chairs so they can sit down.
226. Boys, too!
227. Because he puts down three and carries one.
228. A dentist.
229. Justice (Just-ice).
230. Nothing.
231. One wears an entire costume, and the other wears just a coat and pants (for breath).
232. One has a falsetto voice, the other a false-set-o'-teeth.
233. One sees the plow, and the other plows the seas.
234. One is sworn in, and the other is worn out.
235. The thermom-e(a)ter.
236. Because they like to have their cause (caws) heard.
237. Nothing.
238. Dates.
239. Because it is Nero (near O).
240. So it won't catch cold and become a little horse (hoarse).
241. A mirror.
242. It is fur (far) from one end to the other.
243. He starts on a small scale.
244. Because both are made for tourists (two wrists).
245. Jonah, because the whale couldn't hold him after he got him down.
246. Your calves.
247. One longs to eat and the other eats too long.
248. Because it was too hot to sit down.

249. When the person who buys it weighs 125 pounds.
250. Neither! 5 plus 4 are 9.
251. Because twice ten is twenty and twice eleven is twenty-two (twenty, too).
252. Oh, that! That's Sixty-second Street.
253. A noise.
254. In case he makes a hole in one.
255. What can you expect with so many rocks for its bed?
256. When it is only half-tide (tied).
257. When he comes for sugar, because he settles on the spot.
258. A cowslip (cow's lip).
259. Your nostrils, two for a (s)cent.
260. The nose.
261. Because you hear both sides.
262. Because he knows his keys.
263. Because it is full of currants (currents).
264. It has no head or tail, but a foot at each end and one in the middle.
265. When it's condensed.
266. When it strikes one.
267. Tea (the letter "T").
268. A milking stool.
269. So that he could get rich milk.
270. Then ask the kernel (colonel).
271. When he took a hack at the cherry tree.
272. Because it has been re-seated (receipted).
273. In the hatchway.
274. Because it grows down.

275. The sausage-maker, because he makes both ends meet (meat).
276. Because it has a head and a tail and two sides.
277. In your pocket, your cash pocket, of course.
278. Because it is hard to fill.
279. Her chauffeur.
280. Because it suits (soots) him.
281. Let it rain.
282. It is full of figures.
283. Out of the hole, to be sure!
284. One cannot see to go, and the other cannot go to sea.
285. A true balance or a pair of scales.
286. A secret.
287. One is too thin, the other tooth out.
288. Because he should never sleep on his watch.
289. If you will be pleased with what you have.
290. Because it makes candles (scandals).
291. Because they are opposed to the motion.
292. Sleigh (slay) it.
293. Because there is so often an evening mist (missed).
294. Sealing wax.
295. Sense.
296. Because she often has to be told (tolled).
297. A shadow.
298. Because she has an eye for each of them.
299. Because he has a bare (bear) face.
300. The bus fare.
301. Because he had the hives.
302. Dentis-try (tree).

ANSWERS TO RIDDLES

303. Makes a night of it.
304. February—it's the shortest.
305. Because they are longer in bed than others.
306. Because he makes lines.
307. Because the minutes are not (h)ours.
308. When it can't bear you.
309. The tongue of your shoe.
310. March 4th (forth).
311. The price of a ticket.
312. Tree, mend us! (Tremendous!)
313. Oil it!
314. Use the spur of the moment.
315. The receipts (re-seats).
316. Because it comes peal (peel) on peal (peel).
317. Vacci-nation, because it is almost always in arms.
318. To make the tomato ketch-up (catch up).
319. Truth crushed to earth will rise again, but eggs won't.
320. B-head it.
321. Just by telling the bare facts.
322. A corn (acorn).
323. Because it stops at the sound of woe (whoa).
324. Because it can never be-long to you.
325. At any re-tail store.
326. A shoe.
327. One ducks the shoes and the other shoos the ducks.
328. When it is on a clock.
329. Two shoes.
330. When he is heeling (healing).
331. Because he is a man of size (sighs).

332. Because she deals in precious (s)tones.
333. A nutmeg-grater (greater).
334. When it is smoked.
335. When he cannot help it.
336. No one nose (knows).
337. A uniform.
338. When he is in quarters.
339. No, only once.
340. To make it more striking.
341. When it is a little pale (pail).
342. To wake curly in the morning.
343. Because she goes with loaded arms.
344. When she has hazel eyes, chestnut hair, and is married to a colonel (kernel).
345. Wrinkles.
346. Tell him, "That's *some* lyin'!" (lion).
347. One is signed and dated, and the other dined and sated.
348. Wallpaper.
349. Sixteen nights. (One ear of corn and his *own* two ears each night!)
350. Spellbound.
351. "Well, that beats (beet's) all!"
352. Because it's too long to go around them.
353. Because she brings in the clothes (close) of the week.
354. 19-$\frac{1}{2}$.
355. Never lend your books.
356. Because he had a bark (barque) of his own.